The Ultimate
Rhinoceros
Book for Kids

100+ Amazing Rhino Facts, Photos & More

Jenny Kellett

BELLANOVA

MELBOURNE · SOFIA · BERLIN

Rhinoceroses: The Ultimate Rhino Book
www.bellanovabooks.com

ISBN: 978-619-92219-2-1
Bellanova Books

Contents

INTRODUCTION

The mighty rhinoceros is one of the most fascinating animals in the world. Its huge size, armoured body and pointed horns make rhinos a beloved animal of kids and adults of all ages, yet, sadly, its future is at risk. In this book, you'll learn more about the rhino's daily life, species, conservation and more. At the end, you can test yourself in our rhino quiz.

Are you ready? *Rhi-no you are, so let's go!*

RHINOS:
THE BASICS

What are rhinos and where do they live?

Rhinoceroses, or rhinos, have been roaming the earth for around 50 million years. Over the years, rhinos have taken on many different forms—some with and some without horns. Nowadays, we have five species of rhino, all with horns.

• • •

The extinct woolly rhinoceros lived across Europe, North Africa and Asia around 5.3 million to 11,700 years ago. It was huge

with two horns and a very woolly coat.
Rhinoceroses belong to the family
Rhinocerotidae, and within this family,
there are five species of rhinos, which we
will look at later in the book.

• • •

Today, all wild rhinos live in Africa or Asia.
However, they also used to live in Europe
and North America. In fact, rhinos were
the most common large herbivores in
North America until around five million
years ago when climate change wiped
them out.

Indian Rhinoceros   >

Rhinos are **odd-toed ungulates**, which means they are four-legged mammals with an odd number of toes. This puts them in the same category as horses, zebras and tapirs.

• • •

Rhinos are part of a group of animals called **megafauna**. Zoologists use this word to talk about animals that are the largest in their ecosystem, and usually don't have many predators. Other megafauna include elephants, hippopotamuses and large bison.

African rhinos mostly live in savannahs and shrubby areas, while Asian rhinos live in rainforests in tropical areas. The one thing they have in common though is that they can always be found near a good source of mud!

• • •

The word rhinoceros comes from two Greek words: *rhino*, meaning nose and *ceros* meaning horn.

• • •

Male rhinos are called **bulls** and females are called **cows**. Young rhinos are called **calves**.

A crash of white rhinos.

A group of rhinos is called a herd or a crash.

• • •

The plural of rhinoceros can be either rhinoceroses, rhinoceros, or rhinoceri — take your pick!

• • •

Rhinos live long lives—usually around 45-50 years in the wild. In captivity, they may live even longer.

• • •

The world's oldest Sumatran rhino, Bina, lives at the Sumatran Rhino Sanctuary. She is 42 years old and very shy.

GEOGRAPHIC RANGES OF THE
FIVE LIVING SPECIES OF RHINOCEROSES

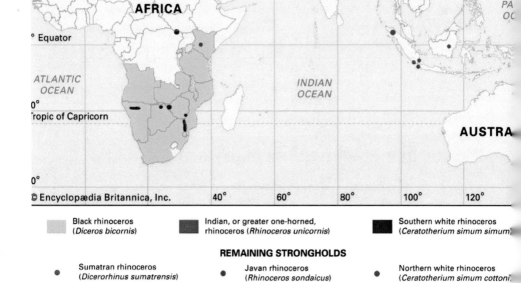

	Black rhinoceros (*Diceros bicornis*)		Indian, or greater one-horned, rhinoceros (*Rhinoceros unicornis*)		Southern white rhinoceros (*Ceratotherium simum simum*)

REMAINING STRONGHOLDS

	Sumatran rhinoceros (*Dicerorhinus sumatrensis*)		Javan rhinoceros (*Rhinoceros sondaicus*)		Northern white rhinoceros (*Ceratotherium simum cottoni*)

Credit: Encyclopedia Britannica.

Rhinoceros Species

There are five species of rhinoceroses—two live in Africa and the other three live in Asia.

Let's take a closer look at the differences. Afterwards, see if you can identify all the different species in the photos in this book without looking at the captions!

White Rhinoceros

Ceratotherium simum

The white rhino is the largest species of rhino. They are the most social species and they live in crashes or herds of up to 10 other rhinos, usually mostly female with a dominant male.

There are two subspecies—the southern white rhino and the northern white rhino. While there are many southern white rhinos living in the wild, sadly, the northern white rhino is critically endangered and may even be extinct in the wild. There are only two female northern white rhinos in captivity, Fatu and Najin—who live in Kenya. The last male northern white rhino in captivity died in 2018.

Southern white rhino.

Northern white rhino. *Credit: Prosthetic Head*

White rhinoceroses live in grassland and savannahs in sub-Saharan Africa. Around 98% of white rhinos live in South Africa, Namibia, Zimbabwe, Kenya and Uganda. Like all rhinos, white rhinos love water and mud and you'll often see them cooling down in a large mud hole.

Despite what their name suggests, white rhinos aren't actually white! Its name is believed to be a mistranslation from the Dutch word "wijd", meaning "wide" in English, as the first explorers named the species after its huge, wide mouth. Their wide mouths make it easy for them to get close to the ground and eat grass.

It's not just their mouths that are huge, though. White rhinos are incredibly heavy—and only just lighter than the largest land mammals in the world, the elephant. Male white rhinos weigh around 2,300 kg (5,070 lb) while the females have an average weight of 1,700 kg (3,750 lb)—that's heavier than a car! If you look carefully you'll also see a hump on the back of their necks, which other species don't have.

Black Rhinoceros

Diceros bicornis

Black rhinos are native to eastern and southern Africa, living in countries such as Angola, Botswana, Kenya and South Africa.

Despite its name, the black rhino is not black—its colour varies from brown to grey. It is believed that the name was chosen simply to distinguish it from the white rhino, the only other rhino species living in Africa.

You can tell the two rhinos apart by the shape of their lips—the black rhino has a pointed, or hooked, lip, while the white rhino has a much wider lip. This is why the black rhino is often called the hook-lipped rhino.

There are eight subspecies of black rhino, three of which are sadly already extinct and one of which is very close to extinction—the Chobe black rhinoceros. The only subspecies not to be critically endangered is the southwestern black rhinoceros.

Black rhinos are smaller than white rhinos and have two horns. The black rhino's hooked lip helps it to grab leaves and twigs off of trees, its preferred food.

Indian Rhinoceros

Rhinoceros unicornis

The Indian rhino, also known as the greater one-horned rhinoceros or great Indian rhinoceros, is native to northern India and Nepal. In the past, they used to live across much of central Asia including Myanmar and southern China.

Listed as vulnerable by the IUCN, there are around 3,588 Indian rhinos left in the wild and in captivity. Nearly 85% of Indian rhinos live in Assam, a state in northeastern India just below the Himalayan mountains.

Indian rhino and her calf.

Indian rhinos have only one horn. They are the second-largest land mammal in Asia after the Asian elephant, and also the second-largest rhinoceros species after the white rhino.

Their skin is thick and grey-brown with pinkish skin folds and wart-like bumps on the shoulders and upper legs.

They, like all rhinos, are herbivores and they enjoy grazing on grass and occasionally eat leaves and aquatic plants.

Javan Rhinoceros

Rhinoceros sondaicus

The Javan rhino, also known as the Sunda rhinoceros or lesser one-horned rhinoceros, is a very rare species of rhino, which lives on the island of Java in Indonesia. Although it looks very similar to the Indian rhino, it is smaller and only the adult males have a horn. Their horns are the smallest of all rhino species and they have a pointed lip.

Sadly there are less than 100 Javan rhinos left in the wild, and none in captivity, making it possibly the most endangered mammal on the planet.

A Javan rhino caught on camera in Vietnam. © WWF/CTNPCP/Mike Baltzer

The only place they live is in Ujung Kulon National Park, a World Heritage Site.

They are solitary creatures and live in lowland rainforests and wet grasslands. Not a lot is known about them as they are so rare, and scientists don't want to risk disturbing them to study them.

Conservation groups are working hard to protect the remaining Javan rhinos, however, they are faced with poachers who kill Javan rhinos for their horns, which can be sold for up to $30,000 per kg—much more than African rhinos'.

Sumatran Rhinoceros

Dicerorhinus sumatrensis

The Sumatran rhino, also known as the hairy rhinoceros or Asian two-horned rhinoceros, is another very rare species of rhino—there are less than 80 left in the wild and around 10 in captivity. It is the smallest species of rhino and lives in hilly parts of the rainforests on the islands of Sumatra and Borneo in Indonesia. However, in the past, it lived across many parts of Asia.

The Sumatran rhino is the only Asian rhino with two horns, although one of them is just a stub. Unlike the other rhino species, the Sumatran rhino has thick reddish-brown hair covering its body.

Sumatran rhinos are folivores, meaning that they survive on leaves. They will eat around 50 kg (110 lb) per day, usually around dawn, after which they like to stay cool in mud baths.

Rhinoceros
Characteristics

Size, features, special traits and more.

Rhinos have poor vision—they can see less than 30 m ahead of themselves—but they have amazing hearing and smell, which is enough to help them get around and find food.

• • •

Rhinos have between 24 to 34 teeth, depending on the species. African rhinos have no teeth in the front of their mouths, instead, they use their lips to pluck food.

What type of rhino do you think this is?
Hint: It has a hooked lip and no front teeth.

White rhino with three
bird friends.

The rhino's horn is made entirely of keratin—the same substance that our hair and nails are made of.

• • •

If a rhino's horn is removed (most commonly because of poachers), it will never grow back. This is different from the elephant, whose tusks do grow back.

• • •

You will often see oxpecker birds sitting on rhinos. They have a great relationship— the parasites on the rhinos provide food for the birds, and the birds warn the rhinos when danger is coming!

Although Sumatran rhinos are the smallest, they are still huge—they weigh an average of 600 kg (1,322 lb). However, white rhinos can weigh up to 3,500 kg (7,716 lb)—that's more than two cars!

• • •

Javan and Indian rhinos only have one horn, while the others have two. Rhinos' horns never stop growing, and a white rhino's horn can grow up to 7 cm (2.75 in) each year!

• • •

Asian rhinos are great swimmers and can easily cross rivers. However, African rhinos are terrible swimmers and they will drown if they get into water that is too deep.

Indian rhinos going for a swim.

Rhinoceroses vary in size from 2.5 m (8 ft) long and 1.5 m (5 ft) high at the shoulder in the Sumatran rhinoceros to about 4 m (13 ft) long and nearly 2 m (7 ft) high in the white rhinoceros.

• • •

Rhinos have very thick skin, which forms folds around the shoulders and thighs that look like armour.

• • •

Rhinos have very sensitive feet! When they walk they put most of their weight on their toes to avoid hurting the sensitive skin on the bottom of their feet.

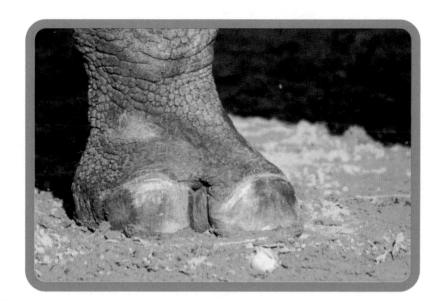

All rhinos are grey or brown in colour, however, the white rhino is usually the palest shade of grey.

• • •

Today, only the Sumatran rhino has hair (other than small tufts on the tails and ears), but this wasn't always the case. Fossils show that all rhinos used to be covered in thick hair!

Rhinoceros calf on the run.

Rhinos have three short toes, which have wide, blunt nails on them.

• • •

For their size, rhinos have small brains. They're not the smartest animals, but what they lack in intelligence they make up in sheer size, which helps keep them safe from predators.

• • •

Rhinos are fast when they want to be! They can run at speeds of up to 30-40 miles per hour (48-64 km/h).

Rhinos: Their Daily Lives

What do rhinos do all day?!

Rhinos spend most of their days, especially when it's very hot, wallowing in mud. This helps keep them cool and protects them from parasites and insects, as well as making sure their skin stays supple and doesn't crack. The dry mud also provides protection from the sun.

Rhinos *love* mud!

Rhinos can be divided into two different eating styles. Black, Javan and Sumatran rhinos are browsers, while the others are grazers. Browsers eat leaves, twigs and fruit that are above ground, whereas grazers munch on low-lying grass.

• • •

It takes a lot of plants to feed a rhino! They eat up to 54 kg (120 lbs) a day to sustain their large bodies.

• • •

Most rhinos are quite territorial and can get aggressive if other rhinos come into their space. They mark their territories using dung and urine. The piles of dung are called middens.

Rhino and her calf in
South Africa.

A small crash of white rhinos.

Middens are used by male and female rhinos to communicate their whereabouts with each other—and also whether they are ready to mate.

• • •

Black and white rhinos are semi-social, with the males usually preferring to be alone. White rhinos, however, often live in social groups of up to 10 rhinos.

• • •

Indian and Sumatran rhinos are the most solitary, although sometimes females and young will temporarily form bonds.

Rhinos have funny ways of communicating. They use sounds such as honks, sneezes and snorts depending on whether they are happy, scared, angry or alarmed.

If you hear the sound "*mmwonk*" from a rhino, it means it's very happy!

Rhinos, like elephants and giraffes, use infrasonic sound waves that only they can hear.

• • •

Rhinos usually avoid humans, and there are less than two known attacks per year.

• • •

African rhinos are more likely to attack a human if they sense danger, whereas Asian rhinos would most likely just hide.

• • •

The most dangerous rhinos are cows with calves as the mother will instinctively want to protect her child.

Asian rhinos use their teeth to fight, not their horns! An Indian rhino's teeth—which look like tusks—can reach up to 13 cm (5 in) in length. African rhinos don't have these long teeth, so rely on their horns for defence.

• • •

Rhinos love to spray their urine around. Male Indian rhinos can even spray their urine over a distance of 4.87 m (16 ft). Zookeepers need to be particularly careful!

• • •

Rhino farts smell so bad that beer brewers call the smell from the process of fermentation, which produces stinky sulfur, a 'rhino fart'.

Male Indian rhinoceros.

Black rhinos have a higher death rate from 'mortal combat' than any other mammal on the planet. About 50% of males and 30% of females die from fighting-related injuries.

• • •

Rhinos sleep for around eight hours a day, in intervals. They can sleep standing up—but if they need a deep sleep they have to lie down.

From birth to adulthood

Baby rhinos are some of the cutest in the animal world, so let's learn more about the early life of rhinos.

Rhinos don't breed very often, and not until they are relatively old, which is one of the reasons why their numbers are decreasing.

• • •

The **gestation period** for rhinos (how long a pregnancy lasts) is between 14 and 17 months, depending on the species.

White rhino calf
with her mother.

White rhino cow and calf.

Cows can start producing young when they are around six years old, while bulls don't start mating until they are between six and ten years old.

• • •

There will usually be a gap of between 2-4.5 years between calves and over her lifetime, a cow will have an average of 14 calves.

• • •

Like many large mammals, rhinos usually only give birth to one calf. Twins are very rare.

Newborn rhinos start walking just hours after being born, but they'll still be a bit wobbly for a few days!

• • •

It's no surprise that even rhino's calves are pretty big! They weigh around 20 to 64 kg (44 to 140 lbs.) when they are born, depending on the species.

• • •

Calves, like all mammals, drink milk from their mothers—usually hourly when they are very young and every 2.5 hours as they get older. They do this until they are 18 months old, but will start trying out solid food as early as 10 days after birth.

White rhino cow and her calf.

Calves stay with their mothers until they are around two to four years old and are large enough to go out on their own.

• • •

Sadly, tigers kill up to 20% of all Indian rhino calves. However, once they are over one year old, rhinos don't have any non-human predators and their main threat is humans.

< **Black rhino calf with her mother in Kenya.**

Indian rhino and her calf.

Rhinos:
Conservation

What is being done to protect the future of rhinos and how can you help?

Around 100 years ago, there were over half a million rhinos in the wild—now there are less than 30,000. The main threat to rhinos is poachers. Poachers are people who kill animals for money.

When it comes to rhinos, poachers are usually after their horns, which can be sold for thousands of dollars. Many Asian cultures believe that rhino horns provide medicinal benefits, but there is no proof of this.

A rhino in captivity.

According to the WWF, in the last ten years over 7000 rhinos have been killed by poachers for their horns. Poachers are getting very sophisticated and they will sometimes even use helicopters to track and kill rhinos.

Sadly, all five species of rhino are in danger of extinction and the Sumatran, Javan and black rhinos are critically endangered. Today, there are only about 60 remaining Javan rhinos, fewer than 100 Sumatran rhinos, and about 5500 black rhinos.

Thankfully, it's not all bad news! Thanks to the amazing work of conservationists around the world, black and white rhino numbers have increased in recent years.

Many rhinos have been successfully bred in captivity and in general, they live long, happy lives in well-managed zoos.

< **Black rhino at Chester Zoo, UK.**

How can you help?

There are lots of ways you can help protect the future of rhinos. There are organisations, such as the WWF, Save the Rhinos, The Rhino Orphanage, Rhino Force and the International Rhino Foundation that work with rhinos.

Just a few ways you can help:

- Adopt or sponsor a rhino;
- Raise money in your community or at school for rhino conservation projects;
- On your birthday or a special occasion, ask for donations to a rhino conservation organisation in your name instead of gifts;
- Share messages on your social media and talk to friends and family about the problems rhinos face.

World Rhino Day is celebrated each year on September 22, and it's another great opportunity to spread awareness about rhinos.

Check out the websites of the organisations on the left for lots of exciting ways to get involved.

RHINO *quiz*

Now test your knowledge in our Rhino Quiz! Answers are on page 77.

1 Can you name the three species of Asian rhinoceros?

2 What are male and female rhinos called?

3 What do you call a group of rhinos?

4 Which species of the white rhino is the most endangered?

5 Which rhino is larger, the black rhino or the Sumatran rhino?

6   Which species of rhinos have two horns?

7   What is a rhino's horn made of?

8   Rhinos have great eyesight. True or false?

9   Are African or Asian rhinos the better swimmers?

10   How many toes do rhinos have?

11   How fast can rhinos run?

12   What do grazers eat?

13   What are middens?

14   If a rhino makes a "mmwonk" sound, what does it mean?

15 Rhinos often attack humans. True or false?

16 How many hours a day do rhinos sleep?

17 How long is the gestation period of a rhino?

18 How many calves do rhinos usually give birth to?

19 How many rhinos are left in the wild today?

20 When is World Rhino Day?

Answers

1. Indian, Javan and Sumatran rhinos.
2. Males are called bulls and females are called cows.
3. A herd or a crash.
4. The northern white rhino.
5. The black rhino.
6. Black rhinos, white rhinos and Sumatran rhinos.
7. Keratin.
8. False.
9. Asian.
10. Three.
11. Up to 30-40 miles per hour (48-64 km/h).
12. Mostly grass.
13. Piles of dung.
14. The rhino is happy.
15. False.
16. Eight.
17. Between 14 and 17 months.
18. One.
19. Less than 30,000.
20. 22nd September.

Rhino
WORD SEARCH

```
Q E T R E J A S V Z D N
J Y N V E Z A P K T G S
M I D D E N E V J B C U
A U C R A S H L A T Y M
M Y Q H F N S N V N X A
M K Q J F S G N T E A T
A E N K F S A E E H Z R
L R H I N O C E R O S A
S A J E S G W A B E D N
G T D S A Q D Z L B D E
T I E S A J T D W F V H
H N Z Q W H T E S D S D
```

Can you find all the words below in the word search puzzle on the left?

RHINOCEROS   MIDDEN   CALF

MAMMALS   SUMATRAN   CRASH

ENDANGERED   KERATIN   JAVAN

Rhino CROSSWORD PUZZLE

Use the clues below to fill in the crossword puzzle on the right!

Across

4. What rhinos do in mud
6. Black rhino's continent
8. Shorter word for rhinoceros
9. Biggest rhino species

Down

1. Most endangered white rhino
2. Smallest rhino species
3. Another name for the black rhino
5. White rhino's eating-style
7. Female rhino

Word search solution

	E			J							
		N			A						S
M	I	D	D	E	N		V				U
A		C	R	A	S	H	A				M
M				N				N			A
M	K				G						T
A	E					E					R
L	R	H	I	N	O	C	E	R	O	S	A
S	A					A			E		N
	T						L		D		
	I						F				
	N										

Crossword solution

	1 n		2 s			3 h		
	o		u					
	r		m			h		
	t	4 w	a	l	l	o	w	
5 g	h		t			o		
r	e		r			k		
6 a	f	r	i	c	a	l		
z		n			n	i		
e			7 c			p		
8 r	h	i	n	o		p		
			9 w	h	i	t	e	
						d		

Across / Down solution grid:

- 1 (down) **north**
- 2 (down) **sumatran**
- 3 (down) **hooklipped**
- 4 (across) **wallow**
- 5 (down) **graze**
- 6 (across) **africa**
- 7 (down) **c**
- 8 (across) **rhino**
- 9 (across) **white**

Sources

Kenyan northern white rhino Najin retired from breeding scheme (2022). Available at: https://www.bbc.com/news/world-africa-59005006 (Accessed: 22 April 2022).

Facts, A. (2022) Rhino guide: how to identify, where to see and why they're endangered, Discover Wildlife. Available at: https://www.discoverwildlife.com/animal-facts/mammals/facts-about-rhinos/ (Accessed: 25 April 2022).

Sumatran Rhino (2022). Available at: https://www.worldwildlife.org/species/sumatran-rhino (Accessed: 25 April 2022).

Top 10 facts about rhinos (2022). Available at: https://www.wwf.org.uk/learn/fascinating-facts/rhinos (Accessed: 26 April 2022).

Meyer, A. (2022) Rhino Attacks On Humans, Rhinosinfo.com. Available at: https://www.rhinosinfo.com/rhino-attacks-on-humans.html (Accessed: 26 April 2022).

rhinoceros | Horn, Habitat, & Facts (2022). Available at: https://www.britannica.com/animal/rhinoceros-mammal (Accessed: 26 April 2022).

Facts About Rhinos (2018). Available at:
https://www.livescience.com/27439-rhinos.
html#:~:text=Rhinoceroses%20are%20large%2C%20
herbivorous%20mammals,horns%2C%20while%20
others%20have%20one. (Accessed: 26 April 2022).

Fun Facts About Rhinos | Save The Rhino (2022).
Available at: https://www.savetherhino.org/rhino-info/rhino-kids/fun-facts/?cn-reloaded=1 (Accessed: 27 April 2022).

15 Things You Might Not Know About Rhinos (2018).
Available at: https://www.mentalfloss.com/article/541375/
things-you-might-not-know-about-rhinos (Accessed: 27 April
2022).

How Much Do Rhinos Sleep? (2019). Available at: https://
rhinos.org/blog/how-much-do-rhinos-sleep/ (Accessed: 27
April 2022).

Rhino Facts – The Rhino Orphanage (2022). Available at:
https://therhinoorphanage.co.za/about-the-rhino/rhino-facts/
(Accessed: 27 April 2022).

We hope you enjoyed exploring the world of rhinos! If you loved the book, we would be so grateful if you could take a moment to leave us a **review** on your preferred platform. Your feedback helps us improve and create even better books for curious young readers like you.

Thank you for your support!

Also by Jenny Kellett

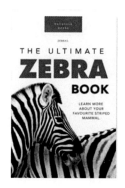  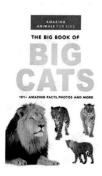

... and more!

Available at
www.bellanovabooks.com
and all major online bookstores.

Made in United States
Orlando, FL
01 January 2024

41952680R00049